For Victor

with

every good wish

Brian

StAnza 2010

The Book of Belongings

Also by Brian Johnstone

POETRY
Homing (The Lobby Press, 2004)
Robinson, A Journey (Akros Publications, 2000)
The Lizard Silence (Scottish Cultural Press, 1996)

POETRY IN TRANSLATION
Terra Incognita (Vincenza: L'Officina, 2009)

AS EDITOR
The Memory of Fields: the poetry of Mark Ogle
(Akros Publications, 2000)
The Golden Goose Hour (Taranis Books, 1994)

The Book of Belongings

Brian Johnstone

2009

Published by Arc Publications
Nanholme Mill, Shaw Wood Road
Todmorden OL14 6DA, UK
www.arcpublications.co.uk
Copyright © Brian Johnstone, 2009
Design by Tony Ward

Printed in Great Britain by the MPG Books Group,
Bodmin and King's Lynn

978 1904614 75 3 (pbk)
978 1906570 15 6 (hbk)

ACKNOWLEDGEMENTS:
Thanks are due to the editors of the following publications in which several of the poems in this collection (or earlier versions of them) have appeared: *Reactions 3, Reactions 4* (both Pen & Inc Press, UEA), *New Writing Dundee* (Dundee University), *Edinburgh Review* (Edinburgh University), *Chapman, Island, Sou'wester* (University of Southern Illinois, USA), *Poetry Cornwall, New Welsh Review, The Red Wheelbarrow, Poetry Greece, The Dark Horse, Acumen* & *Smiths Knoll*. Poems have also appeared in the anthologies *Such Strange Joy* (iynx, 2001), *The Book of St Andrews* (Polygon, 2005), *There's a Poem to be Made* (Shore Poets, 2006), & *Skein of Geese* (StAnza / The Shed Press, 2008). Several of the poems first appeared in the pamphlet *Homing*, published under the author's own imprint, and in his Italian collection *Terra Incognita*, translated by Marco Fazzini, Roberta Cimarosti & Armando Pajalich.

'Some Resort' won the Mallard Poetry Competition in 1998, 'The Home Service' was a prize winner in the Ware Poets Competition in 2005; both poems appeared in the competition anthologies. Several poems have appeared in translation in *Pånytt* (Sweden, 2005, trans. Boel Schenloer); *Poetinis Druskininku rudo* (Lithuania, 2005, trans. Kornelijus Platelis) & *Ars Poetica* (Slovakia, 2006, trans. Marián Andricík).

Thanks are also due to the Scottish Arts Council for the award of a Writer's Bursary (1998) and a number of Professional Development Grants. The author wishes to express his gratitude to Jo Shapcott and John Wedgwood Clarke for their skilful editing; to Will Maclean for permission to use his work 'The Archaeology of Childhood' as a cover illustration; to David Harsent for permission to quote from his poem 'Arena' as an epigraph to this collection; to Stewart Conn, Don Paterson, Michael Longley and Anna Crowe for their help and advice with the poems in this collection; and, as always, to his wife Jean Johnstone for her critical appraisal, her constant inspiration and unstinting support.

Cover image by Will Maclean

This book is in copyright. Subject to statutory exception and to provision of relevant collective licensing agreements, no reproduction of any part of this book may take place without the written permission of Arc Publications.

Editor for the UK and Ireland: John W Clarke

For Jean

Contents

Gable / 11
The Trampy Men / 12
Incendiary / 13
This is a Mono Recording / 14
The Home Service / 16
Bringing Them Home with The Saints / 18
Taking a Letter / 19
Empire Days / 20
Class Photograph / 21
After Mallory / 22
The Commonplace / 24
Terra Incognita / 25
Numismatics / 26
Projection / 27
Belief / 28
My Empty Hands / 29
Trace / 30
Early Photographs of Historic Towns / 31
Like Braille / 32
A Definition of Space / 34
A Reading of Bark / 36
A Proof of the Uists / 37
The March Stone / 38
Firth / 40
The Train Now Waiting / 41
Script / 42
A Condition of the Skin / 24
Flashback / 45
Somme '96 / 46
Passage / 47

Shed Blue / 48
Amber / 49
Growth / 50
Coloured / 52
Solstice / 54
Elements / 55
Ramsons / 56
Crossing the Lagoon at Dusk / 57
A Measure of Time / 58
Homing / 59
On Minos Street / 60
Chez Monsieur / 61
The Man Who Sang to Wine / 62
The Cold Shelf / 63
Snagged / 64
Title Shot / 66
Some Resort / 67
Recall / 68
The Experiment of Dr Beaurieux / 69
The Archaeology of Meso-America / 70
Assent / 71
Sootfall / 72
Kissing the Shuttle / 73
The Contours of the Mind / 74
Crash Site / 75
Place of Graves / 76
The Book of Belongings / 77

Notes on Poems / 79
Biographical Note / 81

"Not everything buried is dead."
DAVID HARSENT

Gable

Long gone, those derelict tenements,
half-demolished,

a row of parlour walls stacked up
like sample cards

for someone's granny's wallpaper. Their slivers,
flapping in the wind,

goodbyes. Unlaid,
their fires all died, burned shadow

black into the grates that stamped each wall
with absence, empty

as some broken jug which stood once –
held the milk, some flowers, loose change

for the meter, warmed the baby's bottle – whole,
on each one of these mantelshelves,

in living rooms complete
with hearthrugs, tables, easy chairs,

the neighbours in to borrow tea, just
floating there.

The Trampy Men

Those trampy men, the real ones,
must have gone around that time: the year
the final tram went by, the tracks were ripped up from the setts.

I'd watched it from the flat, toes peeking from pyjamas,
striped, like those I saw weeks later,
as their wearer, out from the asylum, moved my way.

Just loonies, we said, *tipped into the bin;*
tipped out again to take the air.
We'd spoken to them, laughed at unexplained remarks

that made me fail to understand his wave:
the quick flick of his fingernails – my learning curve.
Broken, ragged, striping blood across my cheek, it stayed,

made these the tracks I ran on now:
to turn and gawp at weirdos, every trampy man,
unshaven, frayed and off the rails. Or daft,

like this, the latest one I'd spied in town:
tin hats some army surplus store had sold him for a bob,
a khaki-hued pagoda stacked upon his pate.

Safe upon the bench seat of the Consul,
I twisted round to stare, to snag the buckle of my Start-Rites,
stripe new ox-blood upholstery, tear at flesh.

Incendiary

He lit them when he could, with matches
from the pockets of his coat, or from the cellar
where the slack lurked, near malevolent
with lust for fire; threw sugar on them

when, damped down, their smoke belched
green and bilious in the chimney's throat,
believed the magic dancing in the blue of flame
that gloried for a moment, faltered, died; stood back

when that trick with paraffin and flung-in taper
made the Rayburn roar, a spirit he evoked
behind the fire box door, slammed shut
to blast the stove alive. Still more

lay in the power to pump the pressure up,
rouse Tilly lamp and Primus to the pitch
of one desire: the rush of heat, of uncreated light,
the burn that made them sing with life;

or mete out death as did the creature he kept
shut up in the shed, a monster red with rust,
all scabbed and scaly, oily in the dark,
and rank with secrets few had seen at work:

weeds withering, consumed like martyrs
felled by fire he wielded – dragon tamer
raking garden dreels – the perishable sacrificed
to this incendiary, this defender of the faith.

This is a Mono Recording

which fades the way that says
it must be playing somewhere still
revolving in the half light

its thirty-three and one third
merging with the rhythm of a pulse
which is someone else's song

lingered on some dog-watch evening
in the confines of a single room
that's seen its better days

its sixties colours chipped to flecks
of browning forties stain
its lamp shades brittle from the heat

of bulbs that popped before
those shelves were taken down
whose lines still show beneath the paint

before this disc was pressed
released and placed in serried racks
for fifties teens to leaf through

ask to hear a bit in ranks
of listening booths and buy
for something in the region of a guinea

take home to disapproval
muted playing past a panelled door
that later would be covered over

flushed in hardboard
coated brilliant gloss like cellophane
stripped from the cover of an LP

lives ago which fade out
in forgotten single rooms
where albums might be spinning still

each revolution someone else's song

The Home Service

The washing swung its arms
from pulleys in the kitchen;

messages were shelved
in pantries, paid for on the tick;

and everything was one
and thruppence, two a penny,

twenty bob the pound.
A different land, the past,

and we, its wandered refugees,
can not explain for love

or money how it was for us.
The changes came like buses

are supposed to, all at once.
We hopped on, swung a bit

from straps, went all the way
until they caught us, ticketless,

our right to stay on board
the present hissing at us

like some foreign station
as you turn the wireless dial

to find you can't receive
the signal like you used to when

the valves lit up, cat's whiskers
shimmied to a different tune.

Bringing Them Home with The Saints

It's some place in the fuzz of static,
in the drub of spinning reels, caught
by happenstance
                or by a sound man,
guessing its significance, who couldn't push
through kisses, back-slaps, hip-hoorays
to reach the source.
                This was an ending
much like its start – that Munich square,
1914, where one to-be-infamous face
stared from the grain of a photograph –
the crowd, hats in the air, one lighter circle
we've all seen, round a head no halo ever
marked out.
           A target, more like.
                            Harder
to find in the soundscape is *our* man,
the bell of his horn sanctifying the notes
in remembrance, or joy that the damned
thing is over, him spared, and bringing
them home with *The Saints*.
                      Bloody few
with a halo, it's true, but we hear them all
marching, the boys who are missing
his solo, their kisses, a share of the skirt.

Taking a Letter
The best upper sets do it.
       Cole Porter

Missing from work, she explained it away
as a family affair. To the family, work was to blame,
wartime posting her south, her stenography skills
just what the doctor ordered.

But not what he said, probing so deep
that it hurt, blaming the thing
on the war, the bad faith it'd induced. But love
had induced her to do it, just like it said in the song.

Friends all said it was wrong, against every code,
but still booked a hospital bed, kept her hidden
when truth swelled the lie. All those letters
she'd taken, bar one, left unread.

The shorthand for gone was *for good*; for adopted
it was *for best*. The letter made it all plain: she won't see
that baby again. It's back to pounding the keys.
The bell rings – the line ends. Understood?

Empire Days

It is the end of empire and still she has not noticed,
sitting silently in classrooms, the comfort
of maps and globes tricked out in pink,
a litany of possession persuaded to her lips.

Time will bring her to an atlas of despair,
certainties mere footnotes, names in brackets
harking back to Empire Days,
to soldiers' caps in creased and folded newspaper,

Union Jacks too grand for anything
but flags. That rust that grew on drawing pins
has pinned her there to scratch out essays,
anxious that no blot disturb the fluid of her thoughts.

The paper slubs on rotes of capitals and dates,
the import-export trade, great men,
exciting her to write long past the bell,
past change and class and attitude; past me

here, taking my position up, the windows shut,
chalk so dry it squeaks across the board,
half noticing the dust I raise in clouds,
is peppering my clothes, is whitening my skin, my hair.

Class Photograph

There's no strange twin at either end of this,
no-one has run around
behind the straightened backs
to take a rise out of the camera's slow pan:

the only likeness here's each dogged frown
staring back, beetle-browed,
out of the sepia'd past
where someone has failed to take care.

Through one third of the print, a tear
rips a shoulder from one,
a leg from another, breaks their ranks
with an insolence none would have dared.

They're slated for this, split pupil from pupil
by all that the dominie knows,
wielding his tawse;
each one of them stopped in his place,

fixed by attitude, chemicals, measure of time,
but gone, like the faces
that blurred as they moved
while the plate recorded their pose.

After Mallory
> *It is not difficult for me to believe that George's spirit*
> *was ready for another life.*
> Ruth Mallory

Strung out like votives on an icon, below
the Yellow Band, they search the mountain

like a crime-scene, for a clue. A half hour
from the highest of the camps, they find it,

face in prayer, buried in the shale, fingers
clawing at the gravel with a vengeance

he would never have: the English corpse.
Name tag stitched on what the weather left,

fibres winnowed from the shirt are proof
enough. Like breath, the question hangs

condensing in the chill. Did this cadaver
make the summit, focus, take the shot?

The search picks wool from layers, rope
from rough abrasions on the waist. It finds

no camera to bring him back. In thin air,
something close to hope evaporates.

Some tokens from the jacket's folds
are all they take, then lift a cairn to lay

upon the desiccated flesh that slid off,
caught and held. What's left they give

the mountain with a psalm. Unproven,
this is just remains again, a bag of bones

until, ten thousand feet below, hands
receive each object, turn it to the light:

a box of matches, faded Swans; his knife;
his altimeter, smashed and dumb; papers

in a wad he carted, absent-minded to the top:
a letter in his brother's hand, a bill deferred

till his return. And this is when the breath
seeps back, the bones unite again, the man

steps from the photographs, flesh whole.
From faded cuttings, dotted maps of routes,

he picks his way through rocks, crevasses,
glacial moraine, making for the tent.

The Commonplace

The jar will long retain the fragrance
of what it was steeped in when new.
                                    Horace (Epistles 1)

They're there in every shipwreck,
every trench,
stacked in serried ranks or shattered

by some trauma in the past
that whispers in the ear,
the way the thumb prints round the rim

speak volumes lost
but surely close at hand;
like accident, ill fortune, clumsiness

all waiting round the corner,
hiding in a section under soil
the trowel has failed to pick away, the eye

has overlooked; as with this ship – caught out
upon a reef
low tide exposed so briefly

none had made the shout
in time – that foundered, took in water, sank
to lay upon these silted rocks

some planks, a larder, corked and sealed,
the commonplace,
the musk of honey, reek of resin, wine.

Terra Incognita

It's always plain, that coastline
where the land mass fades to white,
conjecture has a field day

with the mapping pen, drawing
continents of supposition
linking sightings spied for minutes

in weather less than helpful
to their proof. It's here the lines
of longitude converge, the ice is named,

peninsulas snake out as much in hope
of what will be discovered
as in truth. No man is bolder

than the scribe, the cartographic right
to name this strait, that neck
of land, this place unseen

for every monarch he has served,
to raise the flag
on calligraphic poles, ink in a claim.

Numismatics

Each coin is an island, contours of the seabed
the lines on the palm that handled it once,
tossed it for a bet, weighed its content
against needs it might buy off, thumbing
ridges and faults for signs of clipping,
closing a jaw on suspect ground, biting
at the mistrust, the strange qualities of land
first seen in a moment of hope, first tested
as shoreline is broached, a place to take hold
is found, and the coin is rolled across fingers,
named for its value, hailed for the arms
it bears on the obverse,
                                      as the hand now
enfolding it, taints it with sweat, each coin
unique in its possessor, in the one left bereft.

Projection

They've peeled the globe the way
you would a piece of fruit in one,

spread it till the continents bleed,
slipped the severed contours over

emptiness this map's perceived
as ice trod by the feet of men, bent

on exploration. Where no-one stands
is treacherous as ice floes, as suspect

as the tundra's firm disguise, seepage
from the pasting of image on to page.

The atlas, damp with its projections,
believes in solid ground, conjures

Russia, Greenland, Arctic Canada,
grows them like a culture on a slide.

Belief

You once said that your parents believed
the world would be a better place, perfected
by now – the old dream of the left you fell for too,

if in its 60s disguise. Easy to scoff, but who else
had hung Hume in their lobby, mixed
Tribune with 78s, Carnegie Hall with the Webbs,

and those *Thinkers* editions, grown weary with dust
in some second-hand bookshop by now. Like
your mother, marked down, her brain foxed, left

on the shelf. Although it is all in her mind
that the pages misorder themselves, the index
degrades – her belief becomes something to fear;

which you do, knowing a mind as alert as hers was
has absented itself, made off to distopian ends,
secure in beliefs which convince her

she's lame. She is not. She's stuck on the page
in some footnote she wouldn't admit, and waiting
for the world to come right – then she'll run.

My Empty Hands

The fire sulks, choked up with wood ash
my reluctance to go out on such a day
of rain and wind, has left to lie there in the grate.

Instead, a steady wash of smoke is rising, ghostly
to the chimney's throat, a memory
of what gave way when we discovered that

we could not get you back, could not get
the wisp of breath, too weak
to spark, to snap back into flames.

But logs like these will work, will make
a fire. I take the poker in the hand
that held your fingers as they gathered cold,

pass its shaft below the fire grate's ribs. Flames
leap back in an instant, enfold
the smouldering wood with what I need: a fire

for the night. Your days have flickered out
as simply as the murmurings of flames
I hear as, reaching out, I warm my empty hands.

Trace

It was a misapprehension of shape. No body bag,
just our duvet, rolled up on the floor, and lying to me,
as your chrysalis-like sheet had done in a different room
late in the day you ceased being my father.

Deceitful, it caught my breath and threw it back
two deaths ago, to eyes surprised they didn't cry
as shaking fingers folded back a neat hemmed edge of cotton
to your chin, unshaven, your face, sunk cheeked and empty

as I felt looking at the husk of you, and finding
nothing more. But now I want to meet you here again,
unroll this quilt, spool back to what we should have shared
with time and patience, pick the stitching out.

My father, you were rolled into that sheet before
my hand had eased its grip. I cannot feel
your fingers in my palm but only absence, the impress
of a word in pencil someone's accidentally erased.

Early Photographs of Historic Towns

What we recognise are buildings
scarcely changed, the houses that survived
in streets whose strangeness we ascribe

to history, their emptiness mistaken
for evidence of life lived at a difference pace
in pasts we think we understand

fixed in black and white. Time, it's true,
has played its part, wiped people wholesale
from our view; left only absence

or a blur that might have been
a dog, a cat – and here and there the sense
of something verging on the human:

a smudge, some captured light, the ghosts
of bodies tricked out of existence,
gone about their business in a mist of haste.

Like Braille

In years the house was tied to land, each day
they'd throw the ashes out,
shovel night soil from the privy,
riddle off accumulated dross

and dump enough of it, it seems,
to harry out the grass,
kill off the campion and vetch
that seed the back lot and the wood,

all apart from this one corner,
rank with nettles, hogweed, gritty underfoot,
black with clinker from the range
they'd never suffer to go out.

It's here a man,
when prodding at the surface with a spade,
will turn up shards and snapped off corners
of a life dead fifty years;

the pots and jars and bottle tops
still tellingly familiar
from the brands that chance brought forward
to his childhood,

the loyalties that managed to cling on
into the time he overlapped,
the way this life,
that turns up tangled in the roots of weeds,

did not. It rusted shut
like all the tins left rotting in the soil
that cannot be forced open,
cannot give a whiff of what's inside

but still might drop a hint at from their shape,
from something barely noticed
bossed upon the lid
a man might try but fail to read, like braille.

A Definition of Space

Perhaps it is enough to walk along
these edges, gather stones
and send them skimming over water

till each ripple copies and recopies,
spreads still further from your gaze
and the stone sinks deeper,

out of reach. At these places
where the meeting and the parting
are the same, the sands run smoothest;

shores are banked with rushes
whose singularity of line stands sheer
and pencil thin against the space

each interrupts. Until they flower:
a seedhead budding from the stems
whose starkness seemed exact

before the breeze got up, the light changed
in that way you'd often heard about
that brings the distance close to shore;

and you began to notice how things were.
How rush stems paired and danced
in moving air, formed geometries

inclining to each other, held space
the way a pair of hands cups time.
It is enough to know this, see how right

can be the bending of a line,
how integral the angle of these stems
to their perfection. They hold your eye

as, from the shore, you take the gift
you've chanced upon; thinking simply
that the stone, which rests a moment

cool against your palm, must be
as perfect too; that it will find the water
fitting to its temper, move across the surface,

will not cease. And in the endless light
of June, you crouch down at the lakeside,
make the throw. It goes and goes.

A Reading of Bark

This is a script to hazard a guess at,
a language of skin and growth
shifting before the eyes, unobserved.

The little we read
from knife cuts, twists of wire,
the necessary nail hammered home,

translates to a human scale,
preferring years
to the centuries bark has sheathed each tree.

Behind this ring a rope burn has left, is time
for the washing to dry,
the garments to fade, be passed on

beyond derivation. Which is there
for the taking alone
in these nicks, intrusions in bark,

these laughter lines, birth marks, scars,
like this set of initials, thickening with age,
rehearsing a future in stone.

A Proof of the Uists

No pencil, ruler, mapping pen
could graph these islands the way

light and shadow,
scrolling their profile along the horizon,

show them today. Current and tide race,
cumulus, stratus

texture the page they glide upon,
while sunlight – sea reflected – streaks

like bog cotton tugged in the wind,
cutting the lines which swell

to peak after peak, each its own
distance away. Their bulk,

distilled to a thread
of low and lochan herded shore,

lies like a strap of bladder wrack
along the world's edge. The pilot pen

steers the eye, draws the line across
the pupil and the iris, bites it, etches in.

Vaternish, Isle of Skye

The March Stone

> *The march between the Shanwell and Old Muirs salmon fishing is in a straight line from the top of Norman's Law to the low water. This march stone stands in said straight line. 1794.*
> Inscription on Fishing Marker

Take time to stand here by this stone,
feel the sandy loam go down for yards
beneath your boots, and listen to the silence,
to the susurrus of sea away to east

where this line threads its route
through pines, through bent, across the dune slack,
all the shrugged up sandhills of the coast
to zero ground, sea level

where it makes its mark, imagined
on the wet sand of the beach: a terminus
here settled by the law. And this time
turn to west, search keenly

through the trunks, the tangle of the forest,
for that hill whose shape you know, but cannot spy
from here, the one these picked-out words
say marks the farther end of this,

the dimly-minded boundary
one stone has been erected to maintain.
Imagine it, invisible but paid out in the thought
of netsmen, pilots, players of the line

they wound from pole to pole,
just as this border knots each bield and brae face
straight – the way a gull flies inland –
heading for the summit of The Law

these trees grew up to hide. One stone,
its legend carved for anyone to read,
that must have stood here, closer to the shore
two centuries ago,

before the sands moved, changed
the angle of the coast, took fish and men away,
to argue other boundaries,
to seek a different Eden, out beyond the Tay.

Tentsmuir Forest, Fife

Firth

Think of the face of the estuary, far out,
beaming with space, open armed
in the sense of a mother, a welcoming friend.

Think of it peopled with craft, each one
a world in an envelope clamped to the waves,
and moving, moving. Out there

they look back at us, know us
as home, a place to put in for the night,
reckoning time since they rounded The May,

and turned to the shore, where we link
light to light, a chain of habitation
gilding the places maps tell us are there.

Think of their people, in houses, the telly on,
that one chair empty and still
for the Firth's release. Its waters darken,

eyes practised in knowing pick out
a headland, a bank, the bruise of a scaur
make ready for port in ways we can only guess at.

Think of them pushing the rope of their wake
back of the stern, clicking on light
in the wheelhouse, steadying, throttling down.

The Train Now Waiting

With the old railwaymen... it was part of your life... railways went through the back of your spine like Blackpool went through rock.
       The Ballad of John Axon (BBC Radio Ballads)

There you go once more, placing
your foot on the plate, pulling
at levers. This fire is firing up your days.

Watch the clock. Pitch its numbers round
inside your head. Believe it, passing
over those beams, rubbing gabardine to a fine gloss

where there is nothing now, space
filled with bramble, dead nettle, the detritus
of late shoppers, drinkers on the lam.

Nothing new. And you unlikely to stop,
stationary in your boots, a waxy sheen. Your place
on the footplate: what was it? A dream?

Script

He'd tie them by their necks
with binder twine
his father slipped him from the shed,

watch mouse flesh stiffen, give up
what he knew of life
suspended from the fence: each skeleton

a minuscule perfection.
And later, with the rats,
whose worm-grooved tails a half-inch tack

fixed limp outside the byre,
he'd study transformation, till each
tined incisor grinned.

In growing up with vermin – weasels, stoats
and more – he'd learned them all
the hard way, strung up on a wire:

the thieves that flanked the killing ground
of Christ, the hoodie crow
they'd pinned spread-eagled on a rail

and planted in the margins of the yard.
There worms diced
meat and muscle for his robes,

the alpha and the omega,
each quill a black and feathered script,
his writing on the wall.

A Condition of the Skin

In one hand warts and tarry string
the other
        fronds of baccy
nails all black
            with one more worry
no-one could disclose.
            Just take a length
and tie it on
        right there
around the root and stump
            and it'll
    whiten
    wither
    die
        drop off.
           Break
the promise with the past
            it ties us up
in knots we had forgotten.
            Like
the woods he kept his den in
        one
        more
        reason
why we had
        to give it up
            whiten
            wither
            cry
                lay off.

Flashback

Roadside tributes flash back light
distracting drivers at the point of impact,

sun careening off the cellophane
that wraps each bunch of dying flowers

laid out on the verge
some vehicle has trenched,

tread-marks etched into the grit:
two muddy scars

which draw the eye
with that inevitable sense collision has

in minds of drivers, hands clasped on a wheel
that spins beyond control

in flashbacks, waking nightmares, even
as it holds a steady course.

Somme '96

Up there on the stone work, unbidden
the names form ranks. Below, the few
who can stand unaided stiffly salute.

Poppies blow in the hedgerows, papery
in centenarian skin. Watery eyes gaze
and in the crowd, a wheelchair creaks.

This is their last trip and they were here
only yesterday. Grasses bend in the wind,
flick back like the pages of a closing book.

Passage

Always it is evening. He will see her,
head tipped to the side, on her face
that look of perseverance, lips in animation.

And he will wonder what it is
she is saying, out there in the summer dim,
telling the stone over and over

something of consequence. Even if curiosity
does not impel him, he will stoop,
read the name engraved upon the surface,

note the age, the year, make a quick calculation
of time elapsed. It is a time. She will return,
maybe next month, maybe the next.

He will have raked the leaves, burned them all
in heaps and cut the lawns one last time
before the winter. She will appear,

a crumpled bunch of roses in her hand.
And he will fumble with the latches,
wonder where he put that oil he bought,

take steps to ease the closing of the gates.

Shed Blue

Based on ultramarine which was synthesised in 1828, this blue distemper covers the walls in The Bothy at Calke Abbey – now much faded and discoloured.
          National Trust Garden Paint Catalogue

They conjured this from base ingredients
in time to have the photograph preserved
in black and white: not quite what was deserved

but light reflecting anyway, and since
they had to make their mark it was enough
to have it noted, if as no more than

the back drop to a rustic scene, this ham
arrangement of the stable boy, a trough,
a wooden bucket and a brush outside

The Bothy. This is where it all became
so clear this shade would never glow again
but be discovered where it first was laid

on walls, which shed it now, a faded skin,
and measure time in flakes:
                              so blue, so thin.

Amber

This stuff could be the memory of time,
the sleep it rubbed out of its eyes
to catch a flake of skin, an eyelash
hundreds of millennia ago.

The look it saves is frozen, glazed,
its meaning held suspended
like beauty nesting in the hand
as lightly as the sunshine it contains.

And more: this beeswing flew in forests
that since were hewn as coal,
trod air exhaled by mouths that now
are fossils chipped from rock,

just as each glob of amber sheds accretions,
takes a polish, turns our stare upon an eye
whose lens was focused on a world
before the spark of us had burned.

Growth

This is the time you give the lawn
its final cut and mow up what
the first cold winds have dropped,

control the old growth with the new
– the last grass, fresh dead leaves –
and roll the season backwards as you go;

the way the clock has just ticked past
the same hour twice; the views you've missed
have shouldered through the trees;

precisely as the night has given more
in taking back the day, its light
distilled to reds of berries, white of frost,

to ambers in the drifts of leaves
which billow, congregate in corners,
crackle dryly like the fires

that someone always lit across the way;
whose smoke we followed when,
as kids, imaginations hot upon the trail,

we found the seasons summarised
in flame, beyond our grasp,
our prize the whole idea of fire,

its unpredictability, so like
the grown-ups under whose control
we were, and it appeared to be.

Coloured

They said the summer wouldn't end,
sugar in the cells of leaves
would take

the gold of sunshine
on into the fading light that waits
as days shrink into months

each growing syllables
like dark. It's still here, though the nights
draw in like counterpanes,

breath condenses in the air
the way a mind fogs with the cold,
while brightness, warmth, fecundity

are merely
pantomime deceits,
the rouge that cuts the pallor on the cheek

of birch and rowan, hawthorn, beech
found out by this contender:
snow. October enters with the cold

insistent as this white stuff melting
rapidly to slush
that quits in no more than an hour

but promises another call,
another and another, white on white
until the colour

drains from everything
save cheeks, the lobes of ears,
or hands held out insistent to the fire.

Solstice

It's the line that's crossed
from the shaded ground
where frost holds north of the dyke,

to its further march
thin sun has lit, and thawed
in the hours these days have docked,

making this
the border all must pass,
step over blindly, blowing on hands.

Elements

Though there's just enough ice to walk upon
we don't
but tread the stiff earth thick with frost,

flip stones
across the surface of the pond
and guard ourselves

from something that those swans must understand,
swimming in the one remaining pool
we try to reach

with bread scraps, loaf heels –
bits of manna from the table – falling
ludicrously short

of our intentions,
our capacity to risk a foot upon the ice,
its bleary depths a veiled uncertainty:

the element
that we forgot to take account of, reckon
as the paper bag was filled,

scrunched shut,
its membrane wiser than the lot of us,
and just enough.

Ramsons

Silence is made greater
in the pungency of these woods,

abandoned
in this reek, the musky green

boots crush beneath each leather tread,
drawing it about the trespasser

like skin. Each year,
forgotten in the hush of winter,

its *droit de seigneur*,
garlic's tenure of the soil, is exercised

in dark. Suck deep,
as it has done for seasons past account,

on leaf mould, worm cast,
humus forming around the root,

and let the quiet breath,
the taste of generations, seed the lungs.

Crossing the Lagoon at Dusk

There should be no sound
but the thrum of machinery stitches her
to the nap of the lagoon.

Piles tack each hem
like common pins,
as the keel shears the channel apart.

Everywhere poles beyond count
fade to the edge
as she shimmers past,

ripping this sheen of silk brocade,
material to both
the water and the dusk.

If this were hand stitched
she'd be oared along,
the twist of shaft in shallows

ruffling sediments
unbroached for years, a velvet darkness
mimicked in the surface

blades are cutting now
to take her where the needle's
steady prick and pull will not go again.

The Burano ferry, Venice

A Measure of Time

A line's been grooved into the flags
that floor this hall with, it seems, as little effort
as its twin inscribed in sand,

though this line stayed,
described its purpose with precision wall to wall
through empty now, but once embattled space.

The hours have hung upon it longer
in this place of pain, than would their like
on any sunlit slab or cloister wall;

hours that poured out into days like all
the potions, salves and ointments charity has used
to shore against despair.

Each rising of the sun has proved that light
would edge along the scale and hope would enter,
measured only by the breach men cut

with this intention high upon the apex of the wall:
that time, God given, might be seen
to seep, like waxen balm, across the floor.

Hospice Hotel-Dieu, Tonnerre, Burgundy

Homing

Although the dyke would seem to point her back
to where the walk began,
she's lost

until these swans wing into view, heading out
for somewhere
that this silt has not turned back to land

which they could walk on, she could not
for fear of sinking
to her knees. Her eyes track every wing-beat

as the wind decides their course,
forces them to heel about, to tack against the gusts,
show her the way

determination works. They land on what she sees
as scrubby grass and only later
will identify as water,

fen that would have stopped her in her tracks
which lead now – boots on flint,
impacted soil – the way

the swans flew:
banked, oblique but homing
by some instinct, for the place they left behind.

Blakeney, Norfolk

On Minos Street

Nothing depends on this fruit any more,
these oranges someone has hung on a wire
to keep them from mice

long dead. So many summers
have been and gone, all that was flesh has dried
to these six russet pods slung from a beam

slowly rotting to dust. One touch of the hand
and the rafters part company, shift,
the way all the ghosts that left here

this bag of herbs forgotten on a nail,
that oil can shrouded in rust, this bulb of garlic,
hollow, withered to a husk, just

wandered off. In this house, no more
than two rooms and a yard, flakes of plaster
have dropped, spread like petals

over a mattress that rots on a bed
no-one has slept in for years, laid out,
wreathed in blossom, the scent of neglect.

Anatolí, Crete

Chez Monsieur

Chic once, high style for the 40s,
that they made it to this village,
past the press of post-war ghosts,
a feat alone. Now sixty years on,
their cellophane's crisp with age,
but starch-fresh in their wrappers
they still cram the shelves. No-one
can have felt the need, it seems,
to don so citified a garb, as out
of place as she is, shopkeeper
to silence, her business all gone
dead. She sits on in the gloom,
open to defy this lack of trade;
her stock up on display: a history
of half a century's disdain. Time
has flickered to a stand-still; only
clip-on ties, soft collared shirts,
sock suspenders, sleeve restraints
might speak of something never
quite achieved, slipped sideways
through a worm hole in the wall.

St Privat d'Allier, Auvergne

The Man Who Sang to Wine

is who we're hearing in the basement.
Midnight, and we're taking the back stairs up
to that attic room. Morning,

and he's crossing the yard in sunlight,
his voice lifting once again.
A fragment of some lyric, *chant de Renaissance*

filters the air clear. And this
he gives to wine, to cellar after cellar
of the stuff – a chill runs through it.

Somewhere between a tenor and an alto,
this rosé voice spans
a rack of notes. Each song soaked bottle

opens for our lips. The chill is there, the suck
of grape on land, of some acoustic property
on liquid, flowing now

into our throats, the song dissolving inwards,
taking clarity, the flinty soil,
the element of joy, to tune our tongues.

Clos de Vaulichères, Tonnerre, Burgundy

The Cold Shelf

How long it had formed the sill
we never knew. Clay had curdled through
its veining: nothing more. Still, it kept fresh
all that our hands placed upon it,

harboured the north wall's chill,
the ritual of cold sustaining us. Daily
the milk in its blue striped jug,
eggs from the steading, the butter, cream,

were dressed in its frigid air. Paint
made it part of the furniture, broaching
the marble's edge with each spring spruce up,
till a halo of household gloss

rimmed the slab. The days before power
were its glory. Ringed from the base
of bottles and crocks, its inscriptions
were plenty, its lettering some sort of grace.

Snagged

Let us make man in Our image, after Our likeness
Genesis 1: 26

We leave the table near to midnight.
Later cleared, it gives the game away:

a drift of salt, the crystals poised
against the bread crumbs, flakes of rind

that war for space upon this surface,
catching in the clefts of skin, the rough

of cotton, as we swab it down. Enough
to brush this tribe into the rubbish

men will take to rot in landfill; enough
to trust that one day wood will plane

into a surface welcome to the touch,
will take the glossing of a sponge

unsnagged. We quit the task, pinch
salt grains from our palms, accept

decay is evident and all there is beyond
this thickening of the gut, shines back

from waxed wood, marble's mirror sheen,
wars too for space, a floater in the eye,

until it sticks there, snags the tissue
of the brain, makes us look through all

the surfaces we polish, searching for
our faces, for some deeper, richer grain.

Title Shot

There is nothing but these roads
we drive on night by night,

nothing but this rain
thrumming on the windscreen,

and road-kill littering the verges
we hurtle past,

like an endless tracking shot.
You lay your head upon my arm

each touch a confirmation that the take
is still in focus, the foreground sharp.

Our lights sweep round a corner,
make angles on the ceiling of some room.

I ease my foot back from the throttle,
listen as the engine whirrs, like film.

Some Resort

He will be standing on the bridge
half hidden by the mist. Below, it could be
river, railway line, canal. At any rate,
the clench of steel, or water's blank embrace.

Perhaps I will pass him, taking the dog
by a different route, late, after the pubs are out.
He will turn away. The dog, inquisitive,
might sniff at the hem of his coat. But no more.

I will not see, half hidden by a cuff, his fingers
bleeding on the parapet, his flinch
at every breath, but notice, drawing level,
the aversion of his eyes. That is, if I notice him at all.

All I'll know will be the column in the press
– barely read before another breakfast – a scraping
on the stonework of the bridge, and below,
the leaves, rotting in the verges, disturbed.

Recall

I remember it was dawn, as if in that
was anything unusual. With my eyes fixed
straight ahead, I half saw frost upon the ground
and boot soles crushing what little grass was left,

the back of one man's neck, cropped short,
the cap square on the head – and then, as I recall
the squad formed up. The wait, the stone and mortar
which I knew would feel the back of one

who waited also, out of sight, a cigarette
between his lips. And what I wondered most
was how these men, like me, could stand in silence,
watch their breath cloud in the winter air

and know, like me, the task these minutes
held for them. I remember it was dawn. A man,
blindfolded, bound, was stood against a wall;
and I fired wide, that's what I most recall.

The Experiment of Dr Beaurieux

Something that flutters in severed nerves
trips the lids to a random motion, the lips
to rail in silence, convulsed with what
the steel has done. The doctor takes care

in timing the slow collapse to death's face
known from countless darkened rooms;
in raising his voice to a pitch, pronouncing
the murder's name. In the consequent look

is the mark of focus, the grip of a steady gaze;
the hopeless proof which ogles him back,
from its ruff of bloody gauze, past help and him
counting the seconds on the watch in his fist

before lids droop again. The process of science
hangs in the space they inhabit. Something has left.

The Archaeology of Meso-America

This was a bundle of bones long before
it was a boy. Wrapped in the shawl
of a womb, contained, perhaps

at such a moment marked
for what has brought him here: his death,
the sacrifice of flesh. We feed on this:

the past, that room beyond the gallery
hollowed from the rock. And there,
in galaxies of dust, deliver these:

a leather bracelet, brooch of pumpkin rind,
the bag that held his torn-asunder limbs;
the wonder and revulsion of it all.

Men say: we must step back, retreat
from our beliefs, understand his blood,
absorbed into these shreds of bark,

was burned for light, for life, in this,
the hollow of his skull, sliced through,
we see, to taste the substance of his thought.

Assent

Men tied these cords round bundles
of themselves, round gear and harvest,
bare possession, stuff. Hitched rawness
to the skin, bound tracks of rope and line
into the flesh, knots holding purpose,
sacrifices of their sex. Their being
burnt like tar about its ends.

With every climb, each gathering
to the hearth, a deeper cut, one firmer
in the hand, within the muscle of the arm.
Each pace the line held, each the cord
brought goods and chance discovery,
the step still firm. Hemp and sisal,
twisted straw: a guarantee, a bet.

The Whaligoe Steps, Caithness

Sootfall

It dropped into their hands out of the soot,
this token of the past, now stiff with age.

The leather hard, the lace long burnt away,
they held it up, a blackened child's boot.

Today, perhaps a boy of six could force
his foot in here; two centuries ago

a ten year old might even fit this sole
abandoned in the flue, lost in the course

of haste. Into the stack, his knuckles raw,
the threat of fire to goad him from below,

he must've let it lie, and scaled the dark
desperate to move, to sweep away the work,

the boot still on the other foot, they say,
his master always there, a cry away.

Kissing the Shuttle

There was never any reason
not to place your lips against the wood:
crowd-pleaser, you could do it

every time, could draw it out,
a white fleck
gummy on the surface of your lips;

the surest way to speed the loom,
to grow the pennies
in the hollow of your purse.

Inhaling more than any bargain
struck when you clocked on,
you learned too late what grew in you:

the kiss of fibre, staple's pricking breath,
seed you bolted down
from every shuttle's oily stem.

The Contours of the Mind

The cave retains its secrets still, the ones
I probe with fingers laid on every ledge,
sneaked into every crack.
                        It's hopeless,
but he might have left a scribbled note
secreted in the rock – some hint to say
that *I* was his last thought;
                            not duty,
even less the contours of the mind
scientists explore with rubber paste
poured into every crevice of the skull:
enough to cast in plaster how the brain
that rotted from its bone millennia ago
shaped up against the rival they think
gained the upper hand – as if to find
a trace of final thoughts,
                        as lost as those
I seek, but *he* had no time left to leave
and, outmanoeuvred, faced the men
who had him shot.
                    The hand can read
enough to make out meaning just
from what is tangible alone. I reach in,
force my fingertips to understand.

Crash Site

We'll never know if this was merely random,
the chance, in all that ocean, of an island
tearing out the undercarriage,

spreading on the carapace of moor
that clings to what there is of this bleak clifftop,
guts of wiring, bones of brass and steel.

If this was seized as one last possibility,
all that could be wrested back
from engine failure, loss of fuel,

shot up fuselage that bought it
out there somewhere close to the horizon,
it was rotten luck

that threw this mess of bog and outcrop
up below the wings, planted this collision
deep in silence, curlew cry and mist.

The same that swirls about it now,
these few grey fragments clinging to the edge,
out of sight of habitation, all that's left

not much more than we picked out of the moss:
a shattered round, alive with verdigris,
I buff up on the fabric of my sleeve.

Out Skerries, Shetland

Place of Graves

She knows that she's the only one
for miles. The rattling space
of countryside, the empty plain
unsettling her, the urban Jew,
drawn back to this black soil.

The township's there, the name
still on a wall. Her own, surviving
in some faded list, its spelling
recognisably the same, enough
to trace the lot the house stood on.

She knows before she sees it,
it is gone. They all have, ashes
blown across the plain, a trace
of carbon on the surface of the snow,
hidden under still more recent falls.

In this one place of graves she's found
they linger on, the family name
so worn away it might be nothing
more than wish-fulfilment, hope.
She stoops to smother it with snow.

It reads again, a white script
ghosted by her fingers into stone.

The Book of Belongings

The book of belongings of those found dead
lies open across my lap. I cradle it and look and look,
not knowing what I must find, half hoping to recognise nothing.

Photograph after photograph, page after page
of someone's jacket, trousers, shirt: I'm searching the fabric
for stitches my hand has known, for threads my thumb has pulled.

This book is heavy with more than belongings:
with gestures an arm has left in a sleeve,
with breath filling the breast of a shirt.

I place a plate on a table surrounded by empty chairs.
Each speaks to me in the voice of a husband, a son.
Those found dead are a handful. I sweep away the crumbs.

Notes on the Poems

p. 12 'The Trampy Men' The 'last tram' of Edinburgh's original tram service, ran in procession through the city in November 1956. Setts are squared-off granite cobbles.

p. 18 'Bringing them Home with the Saints' In the recording of crowds on V E Day, a trumpet can be heard; I have imagined it to be playing 'When the Saints Come Marching In'. The Munich photograph shows Hitler in the crowd at the start of World War I.

p. 21 'Class Photograph' A domine is a schoolmaster; a tawse is a leather belt formerly used for corporal punishment.

p. 22 'After Mallory' In 1999 an expedition to Everest found Mallory's body but failed to prove he had reached the summit in 1924. The Yellow Band is a rock feature on the Lhotse Face.

p. 27 'Projection' The Mercator projection gives a false impression of the area of the far north.

p. 38 'The March Stone' Tentsmuir Forest lies between the Eden & Tay Estuaries in north-east Fife. A bield is a sheltered place.

p. 40 'Firth' The May is an island in the mouth of the Firth of Forth. A scaur is a sharp rock.

p. 58 'A Measure of Time' The Hotel-Dieu is a thirteenth-century hospital. Set into the floor is a gnomon which records time by focusing a shaft of sunlight through a gap in the southern wall.

p. 69 'The Experiment of Dr Beaurieux' This was carried out on the head of the murderer Languille, guillotined in 1905.

p. 70 'The Archaeology of Meso-America' In 1997 archaeologists in Mexico found evidence of the Zoque people and the remains of children who had been sacrificed.

p. 71 'Assent' At Whaligoe a 365 step cliff staircase, dating from the 17th century, descends to a beach where small fishing boats landed during the herring boom.

p. 73 'Kissing the Shuttle' Having loaded the yarn, a weaver had to suck the end through the eye of the shuttle, a practice which could pass on tuberculosis or cause cancer.

p. 74 'Contours of the Mind' Based on the Obituary of Lady Maclean. Her first husband disappeared during World War II. Decades later she visited the cave where he had died.

p. 77 'The Book of Belongings' During the Bosnian conflict, for identifying remains found in mass graves, relatives had to rely on Red Cross photo albums showing items found with the dead.

Biographical Note

Born in Edinburgh in 1950, Brian Johnstone has lived in the Fife countryside since 1972. From 1975 to 1997 he worked as a primary school teacher in various Fife schools.

Since returning to writing in the late 1980s, he has published a full collection and two pamphlets, as well as appearing in anthologies and other publications in Scotland, elsewhere in the UK and in Europe and the USA.

Several of his poems have been translated into Catalan, Swedish, Polish, Slovakian & Lithuanian, and published in the respective countries. In 2009 a small collection of his poems in Italian translation was published by L'Officina (Vincenza).

In 2003 he won the *Poetry on the Fringe* competition at the Edinburgh Festival. Previous successes include winning the Writers' Bureau (2003) and the Mallard (1998) competitions, as well as being a prize winner in the UK National Poetry Competition (2000).

In 1998 he was one of the founders of StAnza: Scotland's International Poetry Festival, having previously co-founded Shore Poets in Edinburgh in 1991. He has served as a Director of StAnza since 2001 and has also taught creative writing for the University of St Andrews Open Association and the Open College of the Arts.

Brian Johnstone lives with his wife, the maker of artist's books Jean Johnstone, on the edge of the East Neuk of Fife.

Recent titles in Arc Publications'
POETRY FROM THE UK / IRELAND,
include:

Liz Almond
The Shut Drawer
Yelp!

Jonathan Asser
Outside The All Stars

Donald Atkinson
In Waterlight: Poems New, Selected & Revised

Joanna Boulter
Twenty Four Preludes & Fugues on
Dmitri Shostakovich

Thomas A Clark
The Path to the Sea

Tony Curtis
What Darkness Covers
The Well in the Rain

Julia Darling
Sudden Collapses in Public Places
Apology for Absence

Chris Emery
Dr. Mephisto
Radio Nostalgia

Katherine Gallagher
Circus-Apprentice

Chrissie Gittins
Armature

Michael Haslam
The Music Laid Her Songs in Language
A Sinner Saved by Grace

Joel Lane
Trouble in the Heartland

Tariq Latif
Punjabi Weddings

Herbert Lomas
The Vale of Todmorden

Pete Morgan
August Light

Michael O'Neill
Wheel

Ian Pople
An Occasional Lean-to

Paul Stubbs
The Icon Maker

Subhadassi
peeled

Lorna Thorpe
A Ghost in my House

Michelene Wandor
Musica Transalpina
Music of the Prophets

Jackie Wills
Fever Tree
Commandments